Children's Musical Worlds

A Sempre Conference

Children's Musical Worlds

Sempre Conference, 25 October 2014
Student Day, 24 October 2014
Institute of Education
University of Reading

EDITORS:

Mary Stakelum
University of Reading

Evangelos Himonides
iMerc, Institute of Education, University of London

Children's Musical Worlds

ISBN: 978-1-905351-30-5

© 2014 Mary Stakelum & Evangelos Himonides

Published in Great Britain in 2014
on behalf of the Society for Education, Music and Psychology Research (Sempre)
by the International Music Education Research Centre (iMerc)
Department of Culture, Communication and Media
Institute of Education
University of London
20, Bedford Way
London WC1H 0AL

copy requests
http://copyrequests.imerc.org

British Library Cataloguing-in-Publication Data

A CIP record is available from the British Library

cover image: Wellcome Library, London: Three leaves from a Tibetan musical score used in Buddhist monastic ritual with the notation for voice, drums, trumpets, horns and cymbals.

Contents

Children's Musical Worlds: Introduction and Welcome   10
    Mary Stakelum (Conference Chair)

ABSTRACTS   13

Keynote Address   15
    Professor Graham Welch (Sempre Chair)

PAPER: Online diagnostic possibilities for measuring musical
abilities in Hungarian kindergartens and schools   17
    Kata ASZTALOS

PAPER: The formal/informal frontier: learning and teaching
where two worlds meet   18
    Alison BUTLER

PAPER: Working memory in children's musical practice:
preliminary results from an ongoing research in a Brazilian Child
Symphony Orchestra   19
    *Larissa Padula Ribiero da FONESCA, Diana SANTIAGO, Jonatas
    LEAL*

POSTER: Writing Music Inspired by the Creativity and
Fantasy-World of Children   20
    Shiva FESHAREKI

PAPER: Children's graphical representation of music: Gaining
insight into their musical world   21
    Vicent GIL
    Mark REYBROUCK
    Jesus TEJADA
    Lieven VERSCHAFFEL

PAPER: Miming stories and playing rhythms along with
recorded music   22
    José Carlos GODINHO

PAPER: Exploring children's understanding of music through the use of drawings and interviews   24
  Susan HALLAM
  Tijia RINTA

PAPER: Private musical worlds: inside the minds of tweens and teens   26
  Ruth HERBERT

PAPER: The use of experimental music and classical music in children's composition at of children aged 9–10   27
  Emma HAWKSLEY

PAPER: An investigation into College musicians' musical performance anxiety through selected performance strategies (cognitive strategies, behavioural strategies, and cognitive behavioural strategies) by self-management   28
  Wei-Lin HUANG

POSTER: Voices and connections: a polyphony of perceptions from the remembered childhood musical worlds of retirement-phase amateur musicians   29
  Janette JOLLY

POSTER: Working memory   30
  Catherine JORDAN

PAPER: Musical agency in primary classrooms: The impact of informal learning on 5-6 year old students   31
  Leslie LINTON

POSTER: Music and Talent: multiple intelligences development through music   32
  Francisco José Cuadrado MÉNDEZ

POSTER: What is the backwash effect of instrumental music examinations?   33
  Simon PARKER

PAPER: Teachers' attitudes toward using multicultural musical traditions in pre-primary music activities in Tanzania   34
  Albini Akonaay SARAGU

PAPER: Songs from the crib: toddlers; private bedtime
vocalizations: a collective case study   35
  Meryl SOLE

PAPER: Performance anxiety, self-esteem, self-efficacy and
attitudes towards performance in American, Czech and Balkan
University music students   37
  Ena STEVANOVIC

PAPER: Basic psychological needs satisfaction through
instrument learning in childhood and adolescence: a
retrospective study of professional classical and jazz musicians   39
  Rachel SWINDELLS

PAPER: "Orchestra"- can a symphony really make a change?   40
  Lina TSAKLAGKANOU

PAPER: Portuguese children's musical worlds in the public
schools. Why do some children play and other children listen?   41
  M.Helena VIEIRA

CONFERENCE PROGRAMME & INFORMATION   43

Children's Musical Worlds: Introduction and Welcome

Dear delegates,

We are delighted to welcome you to the SEMPRE Children's Musical Worlds Conference and Study Day, hosted by the University of Reading. The theme of the conference reflects our ongoing interest in understanding more about the various musical worlds created by, with and for children, and in researching aspects of engagement with music in childhood and its impact across the life course.

We received a huge response to the Call for Papers, and we hope that delegates will enjoy the range of sessions scheduled in the programme with presenters from as far afield as Brazil, Canada and the United States as well as those closer to home, including our own graduate researchers at The University of Reading. On Friday, the Study Day provides delegates with an opportunity to come together to work on aspects of their own research project and to interact with others in a supportive environment. We would like to thank Professor Dianne Berry OBE, Dean of Postgraduate Research Studies at the University of Reading, who has kindly agreed to open the Study Day.

The conference on Saturday begins with a keynote panel and we particularly pleased that Professor Graham WELCH, (Institute of Education, University of London) will lead on this, with guest presentations from Dr Evangelos Himonides, (Institute of Education, University of London), Professor Adam Ockelford (University of Roehampton), Dr Costanza Preti (University of Winchester), Dr Jo Saunders (Institute of Education, University of London) and Angela Voyajolu (University of Roehampton).

I would like to thank several people who have made an enormous contribution to the running of this conference, especially Dr David Baker, Dr Ioulia Papageorgi, Dr Evangelos Himonides, Debbie Taylor and Helen Mitchell. I would also like to thank SEMPRE who have supported a number of full- and part-time students in attending this event with SEMPRE Conference Awards.

‖ Mary Stakelum (Conference Chair)
University of Reading

ABSTRACTS

Keynote Address

‖ Professor Graham Welch (Sempre Chair)

Institute of Education, University of London

It is a great pleasure to be invited as a keynote speaker for the SEMPRE conference at Reading on 'Children's Musical Worlds'. Over the past two decades, I have been very fortunate in being able to work alongside a wonderful team of researchers in diverse collaborative journeys into children's musical behaviour and development. It seems appropriate, therefore, to ask key colleagues to share this keynote and for each to provide their own distinctive scholarly and professional insights into a discrete (yet overlapping) aspect of children's musical worlds. Following some introductory remarks, the presentations will be as follows:

Angela Voyajolu (University of Roehampton) will present new data from the Sounds of Intent in the Early Years research (led by Professor Adam Ockelford) into pre-school/first school children's musical experiences and the development of a new framework for keeping track of these;

Dr Jo Saunders (Institute of Education, London) will talk about examples of individual children's instrumental learning, drawing on our research evaluations for Every Child a Musician (Newham LA) and In Harmony (Opera North and Sage Gateshead);

Dr Evangelos Himonides (Institute of Education, London) will share examples of our ongoing longitudinal research into the development of advanced performance skills in female cathedral choristers at Wells Cathedral;

Professor Adam Ockelford (University of Roehampton) will present examples of children's musical behaviour and development in the context of complex needs, drawing on the widespread national and international interest in the Sounds of Intent project;

Dr Costanza Preti (University of Winchester) will provide illustrations of our understanding of children's musical worlds in a hospital context from her extensive research in the UK and Italy.

Finally, there will be an opportunity for the team to answer questions and receive comments from conference participants.

PAPER: Online diagnostic possibilities for measuring musical abilities in Hungarian kindergartens and schools

|| Kata ASZTALOS

University of Szeged, Hungary

Technology-based techniques got increasing attention in early childhood education during the past few decades. Due to the motivational factors and children's interest, technical equipment is useful in diagnostic evaluation too. In our research an online diagnostic tool was developed to measure musical hearing abilities in kindergartens of Hungary. The purpose of the study was to explore the potentials of technology-based assessment and to provide an easy-to-use diagnostic tool for educators. Participants of the study were 5 and 6 year old children (born in 2008) from the south-eastern region of Hungary.

The test was administered through the eDia online assessment platform which was developed for delivering diagnostic tests. Children completed the tasks in their own kindergarten using tablets. They heard musical stimuli and instructions through headphones. The test has a child-friendly appearance and consisted of 34 closed questions (Cronbach's a=.72). The four subtests measure melody, pitch and harmony hearing and an innovative task measures the connection between the visual and auditory modality. The means and standard deviation of the test indicated that the difficulty fitted well to the ability level of children (M=44.67; SD=14.52). The results of the test could be used for fostering children's development. Our measurement tool analyzes children's achievement compared to defined reference points and helps educators to plan further developmental process.

PAPER: The formal/informal frontier: learning and teaching where two worlds meet

▌ Alison BUTLER

Open University, UK

This research initiated from my MA dissertation, *Play, Practice, Progress: Analysing productive music-making amongst formal and informal learners (2013),* in which literature review focused on effective practice in both informal and formal musical contexts, informing a case study of nine adolescents and one adult at Royal Alexandra and Albert School.

This paper therefore begins by summarizing relevant literature including Green, McPherson and Sloboda, relating their theories to the experiences of my own pupils: Whilst there was some crossover between learning approaches amongst the participants (largely amongst 'first-study formal' learners who explored additional musical disciplines informally), the primarily 'informal' learners generally showed more self-regulation and creativity in their individual practice.

A year after the initial study, one of the informal learners has begun individual guitar lessons, prompting further research. This extension to my dissertation theme focuses on the learning approaches used by adolescents seeking to incorporate formal tuition into their existing informal musical worlds, and on the implications that this has for instrumental teachers.

Material gathered through lesson observation and interviews with both the pupil and his teacher is analyzed here, the results of which will be used to evaluate the school's provision for adolescent movement between informal and formal musical worlds.

PAPER: Working memory in children's musical practice: preliminary results from an ongoing research in a Brazilian Child Symphony Orchestra

‖ Larissa Padula Ribiero da FONESCA, Diana SANTIAGO, Jonatas LEAL

Federal University of Bahai Brazil

The aim of this ongoing research is to investigate the correlation between working memory and the structure of children's musical practice. Many studies corroborate with the fact that instrumental learning provides a rich collaboration for child development. Memory and others cognitive processes are involved and interact with music making. Thus, instrumental group performance is characterized as a valuable framework for the formation and development of the child musician. This report presents the study's first research stage, which describes and analysis the musical practice of these children, and includes semi-structured interviews. The analysis was based in *Practice*, by Hallam and Barry (2002), which describes appropriate practicing and learning strategies. We investigated if the children were engaged in metacognition; employed mental practice; approached practice in an organized, goal-oriented manner; studied and analyzed the scores; planned relatively short and regular practice sessions; were intrinsically motivated; and listened to appropriate musical examples. To observe children's musical development is essential to the tasks of music educators. Consequently, this study promotes a propitious environment for the construction of methodological tools that may contribute both to the process of teaching and learning, and to research in the fields of music education and psychology of music.

POSTER: Writing Music Inspired by the Creativity and Fantasy-World of Children

‖ Shiva FESHAREKI

Royal College of Music

Children have the ability to access a fantasy world and to transcend reality without effort. This is an act of pure creativity. I relate profoundly to this approach and it is how I want to compose – without any sense of self consciousness.

I worked with twelve 8 year old girls from Bramley Primary School in Walton on the Hill, Surrey, and asked each of them to write a story and to present it in their own handwriting with an illustration. In response, I composed a piece for each story, inspired by the fantasies within them. I employed graphic scores in 'youthful-styling' that directly referenced their illustrations and their handwriting, as well as scores in conventional notation. I invited RCM Junior Department students aged 15 – 17, to play these pieces and to add their own youthful musical interpretation, in response to the stories and my composition, in the performance.

Furthermore, I aimed to turn this process back on the children and teenagers and to encourage them to stretch their creativity, encouraging them to expand on their imagination and take risks in their creativity, and embrace the idea of expressing risky feelings, in the safety of music.

The result was a portfolio of stories, images, compositions, workshops and performances that have begun a new process, as a starting point of a conversation in the importance of embracing youthful creativity and musicianship. The aim is to promote taking inspiration from children's fantasy-worlds and encouraging it, both to allow the children's musical creativity to flourish, but also respecting its value and contribution to the world of music as a whole.

Society for Education, Music and Psychology Research

PAPER: Children's graphical representation of music: Gaining insight into their musical world

‖ Vicent GIL

   University of Valencia, Spain

‖ Mark REYBROUCK

   University of Leuven, Belgium

‖ Jesus TEJADA

   University of Valencia, Spain

‖ Lieven VERSCHAFFEL

   University of Leuven, Belgium

Over the last 40 years, researchers have set their sights on how children represent music by means of invented symbolic systems as an alternative to standard music notation. In a generic sense, diSessa and associates (2002) described meta-representational competence (MRC) as the full complex of abilities dealing with representational issues. Our study aims at exploring the extent to which an educational program for enhancing students' music-related MRC improves both their constructive resources and their critical capabilities.

To this respect, we set up an experiment with middle school students aged 12 (n = 77), who were randomly allocated to the experimental (E) or control (C) condition, so that E learners, but not C learners, were provided with scaffolding. As part of the educational program, the students were requested to represent a brief sound fragment by means of a design tablet device. A set of 20 drawings was randomly selected among the students' representations, and subsequently analysed by all of them, according to six representational criteria from diSessa's framework. Results showed a better performance for the E students. Theoretical, methodological, and educational implications are discussed.

PAPER: Miming stories and playing rhythms along with recorded music

‖ José Carlos GODINHO

Escola Superior de Educação, Instituto Politécnico de Setúbal, Portugal

The present paper focuses on two listening strategies used in classrooms when children listen to recorded pieces of music: (1) miming stories and (2) playing rhythms along. The main purpose of these strategies is to enhance the musical experience on the awareness of structural relationships within each piece of music and, mainly, on the empathic embodiment of the expressive gestures.

Children's artistic expressiveness seems to be developed between associative representation and realism (e.g. Parsons, 1987; Swanwick, 1988). On the one hand, musical expressive gestures might be associated and shared (Lang, 2009) with memories of diverse life situations, drama, movement, etc., and, on the other hand, they can be appreciated within the technical mechanisms applied in its production, such as the strength of the arms and hands of a percussionist.

Some studies conducted in primary schools have shown that both strategies of miming stories and playing rhythms along with recorded music tend to promote memory resistance of both expressive gestures and structural organisation. There seems to be some positive effects also on musical taste and on the levels of argumentation (Rolle, 2013) used by children in relation to the particular musical pieces.

Parsons, M. J. (1987). *How We Understand Art: A cognitive developmental account of aesthetic experience.* Cambridge: Cambridge University Press.

Swanwick, K. (1988). *Music, Mind, and Education.* London: Routledge.

Lang, L. (2009). *Lang Lang Master Class, Piano.* New Brunswick: Nicholas Music Center. [Video file]. Retrieved in March 2014 from http://youtu.be/K1NkbwoC5MI.

Rolle, C. (2013). *Argumentation Skills in the Music Classroom: A Quest of Theory.* In I. Malmberg & A. de Vugt (Eds.), *European Perspectives in*

Music Education II. Artistry and Craftsmanship (pp. 51–64). Wien: Helbling.

PAPER: Exploring children's understanding of music through the use of drawings and interviews

‖ Susan HALLAM

Institute of Education, University of London

‖ Tijia RINTA

Feynlabs, Volunteer East

Background: Research on children's understanding of music has generally considered children's improvisations, compositions, notations, or their understandings of the emotions portrayed in music. There has been little research focusing on how they understand music when listening to it.

Aims: The aim of this study was to investigate children's understanding of music through the drawings they made and their explanations of those drawings and how they were listening.

Method: 18 10-year-olds participated in the study listening to music from three different genres, classical/ film, jazz, and popular music. After listening to each piece the children drew a picture reflecting how they understood the music. They were then interviewed individually and asked about the meanings they attached to the music, what they paid attention to when listening and at what level of detail, what images they associated with the music, how the music made them feel and whether this influenced their understanding. The drawings were analysed using content analysis, and consideration of colour and size. The interviews were subject to thematic analysis.

Results: The themes emerging related to musical elements, dynamics, images associated with the music, affective responses, events associated with the music, adopting a holist listening style, musical structure, lyrics, familiarity with the musical style, and musical instruments. There was a greater emphasis in response to the classical/film music on musical elements, dynamics, and images associated with the music. For jazz the emphasis was on adopting a holist listening style, and listening to and identifying the musical instruments, musical elements and dynamics. For the popular music the themes were events associated with the music, adopting a holist listening approach, acknowledgement of the familiarity of the music and to a lesser extent musical structure and lyrics. The drawings made in response to jazz tended to be abstract, for classical music concrete objects and for the popular music related to events associated with the music.

Conclusions: The combination of drawings and interviews was found to be a useful means for investigating children's musical understanding illustrating the range of different types of understandings which children may have in response to different types of music.

PAPER: Private musical worlds: inside the minds of tweens and teens

|| Ruth HERBERT

University of Oxford

What is it like to experience music as a teen or tween? Do age, gender, personality and training shape personal experiences of music? Young people clearly use music to negotiate ways of being in the world (e.g. the use of music to frame routines) and experiencing the world (e.g. the use of music to mediate perception). Yet, the study of the subjective 'feel' (phenomenology) of children and adolescent's unfolding, lived experiences of music is still relatively recent. This paper focuses on findings from a three year nationwide empirical study of the psychological characteristics of 10 to 18 year olds subjective experiences of music. This was a mixed-method three-phase enquiry, utilizing semi-structured interviews, diaries of music listening experiences (Total number = 34) a web-based questionnaire (Total number = 511) and web-based listening study (Total number = 84) to tap the phenomenology of everyday musical experiences and examine the relationship between musical engagement and personality characteristics, age and gender. Findings indicate that music affords an important means of self-regulation for young people, and that the adoption of strategies to manage aspects of self and identity is evident in prepubescence. Individuals adopt particular modes of experiencing music (e.g. a tendency towards imaginative involvement or dissociative experience), some of which are age-related.

PAPER: The use of experimental music and classical music in children's composition at of children aged 9–10

❚❚ Emma HAWKSLEY

University of Roehampton

This research compares the effect of experimental and classical music in the compositions of children aged 9–10. Data collection took place in a primary school in south London with 71 children (48 girls and 23 boys) over four months. Data included:

- pre- and post-study responses to Webster's tests of musical creativity;
- written responses to different musical stimuli;
- group compositions made in response to experimental and classical music stimuli, the creation and performance of which were video recorded.

Participants were divided for analysis according to whether or not they have instrumental tuition, to ascertain whether differences in musical creativity might occur as a result of different levels of 'taught' musical knowledge.

This research uses quantitative data gathered through frequency counts of compositional factors such as *the presence of a repeated pitch cluster*, and qualitative data obtained through observation and the analysis of interview responses.

All data have been collected and are now being analysed; the results will be interpreted in the light of the work of Hargreaves, Ockelford, Swanwick, and Csikzentmihalyi.

PAPER: An investigation into College musicians' musical performance anxiety through selected performance strategies (cognitive strategies, behavioural strategies, and cognitive behavioural strategies) by self-management

|| Wei-Lin HUANG

Institute of Education, University of London

Most research on musical performance anxiety (MPA) has explored coping strategies to deal with stage fright (e.g. Buswell 2006, Kenny 2011, Patston 2013, Roland 1994, and Wristen 2013). This study investigates the ways in which a self-help booklet (SHB) supports College musicians' preparation for performance. The SHB comprises methods of reducing MPA through selected strategies that researchers have explored and identified as effective, both from music psychology and sport psychology (e.g. Hatzigeorgiadis 2013).

This paper presents findings from the pilot study. Participants were musicians from conservatoires that have an international standing and are exposed to frequent solo work. Participants were asked to use the SHB over a four-week period leading up to a performance. Data was collected through the SHB and semi-structured interviews after the performance. The results of this study show that all the participants in this research were aware of the selected coping strategies and felt that they were very helpful in preparing for performance, but did had not realized they have previously learned the strategies until they read the SHB. Furthermore, the participants who believe they do not experience MPA report that strategies from SHB can enhance their overall musical performance abilities.

POSTER: Voices and connections: a polyphony of perceptions from the remembered childhood musical worlds of retirement-phase amateur musicians

‖ Janette JOLLY

Institute of Education, University of Reading

Recent work has identified a lack of research into childhood musical experience and its influence on an individual's long-term engagement with music. Scrutiny of related literature uncovers three arguments regarding early musical experience: firstly, the complex nature of musical identity formation; secondly, the inter-relationships between childhood learning experiences and lifelong music engagement; and thirdly, the effectiveness of compulsory music education as promoting a foundation for engagement with music from childhood into adulthood for the ordinary members of our communities.

Providing a platform for the previously little-heard voices of retirement-phase amateur instrumentalists, this qualitative, phenomenological work aims to draw on the music life-learning histories of 10 participants currently engaged in instrumental activity. Rich data concerning their recollections and perceptions of childhood musical experiences and subsequent music learning trajectories are collected through a life story approach implementing two-stage narrative interviews incorporating creative 'Rivers of musical learning experience' as reflective and analytical tools.

By focussing a spotlight onto the myriad factors involved in later-life amateur musician perceptions of early musical experience, analysis of the findings aims to enrich current understanding of the complex individual, social and cultural influences impacting on the musical worlds of young people, together with their impact across the lifespan.

POSTER: Working memory

‖ Catherine JORDAN

University of Edinburgh

Exploring short-term memory through the multicomponent model of working memory (Baddeley, 2000; Baddeley & Hitch, 1974) presents the opportunity to discover the influence of music training and practice on the processing and maintenance of information within such a system. The present study compared musician's performance on melody recognition tasks to non-musicians. In experiment 1A, an auditory recognition task was presented to both musicians and non-musicians, under three conditions: control, humming and singing suppression. Singing suppression had greatest impact to non-musicians performance of the task. A second experiment examined musician's ability to encode a visual melody, transform the visual melody into an auditory melody, after a retention interval of 10 seconds perform a recognition task. Across the three conditions as per experiment 1A, singing suppression showed greatest interference during the visual task. These preliminary results suggest a difference between musicians and non-musicians working memory system. It is possible the phonological loop may be enhanced due to music training, hence musicians superior performance on such tasks, compared to non-musicians. However, to further explore these results, a follow up experiment will incorporate a similar experimental design, under three conditions, control, singing suppression and articulatory suppression with the view to further explore musicians superiority on tests of working memory and also, discover the possible existence of a tonal loop within a musicians working memory system.

PAPER: Musical agency in primary classrooms: The impact of informal learning on 5-6 year old students

‖ Leslie LINTON

University of Western Ontario

This presentation explores the results of a 6-month qualitative case-study of informal learning pedagogy with two classes of grade one students (UK year 2) in an elementary school in Southwestern Ontario, Canada. The purpose of this study was to investigate informal learning practices in music education and to examine their potential as a pedagogical approach within the primary classroom setting.

There were several significant findings, two of which will be discussed in this presentation. The first finding embraces the idea of children as active agents in the construction of their musical knowledge. The results illuminated the development of children's own musical worlds within the classroom, guided by their agentic behaviour and informal learning.

The second finding describes the process of reproduction of childhood culture in the grade-one classroom. Harwood & Marsh (2012) have drawn significant connections between children's playground learning and informal music learning as researched by Green (2008). Adding to this comparison builds upon and demonstrates how children bring their outside experiences into the classroom, thereby creating a new environment for music education. The addition of this new environment suggests that through the interpretation and reproduction of children's musical worlds within the classroom, attributes such as imagination, engagement, and creativity are nurtured.

Green, L. (2008). *Music, Informal Learning and the School: A New Classroom Pedagogy*. London: Ashgate.

Harwood, E. & Marsh, K. (2012). Children's ways of learning inside and outside the classroom. In G. McPherson & G. Welch (eds.) *The Oxford handbook of music education, Volume 1*. Oxford: Oxford University Press.

POSTER: Music and Talent: multiple intelligences development through music

▌▌ Francisco José Cuadrado MÉNDEZ

Universidad Loyola Andalucía

"Music and Talent" is an educational project that aims to use music to contribute to the development of the talent and the different abilities, skills and intelligences of each child. This is a training program based on exploration and experimentation through music, and specially on the multiple intelligences paradigm. The following aspects are developed: musical awareness, psychomotor development, auditory and musical perception, relaxation and concentration, strengthening self-esteem, creativity and group work.

This is a program adapted to the socio-cognitive development of school pupils, initially implemented with children's from three to nine years old.

After two years of activity with Music and Talent project, two studies have been conducted, with the purpose of evaluating the consecution of the proposed objectives. The first one has evaluated the degree of children's self-efficacy in relation to the methodologies employed in the classes. Bandura's self-efficacy concept has been taken as reference, and the adaptation from a validated scale by Ritchie and Williamon in music learning researches has been used.

The second one has been a quasi experimental research, analyzing the increment of creativity after applying one of the methodologies used in the project: a system for learning music language, based on the development of multiple intelligences.

POSTER: What is the backwash effect of instrumental music examinations?

▌ Simon PARKER

Institute of Education, University of London

Within instrumental music tuition, examinations function as a motivating factor for students and teachers. This study explored the 'backwash effect' of examinations, referring to the influence they have on teaching and learning. Conducted within an independent girl's school, this mixed method exploratory case study involved students and teachers, and focused on the relationship between the examination criteria and lesson content. Preliminary findings indicate the criteria were generally not understood, and highlighted concerns that an emphasis on examination criteria during lessons may not support the overarching goals of the teachers. Implications of these findings will be discussed.

PAPER: Teachers' attitudes toward using multicultural musical traditions in pre-primary music activities in Tanzania

‖ Albini Akonaay SARAGU

University of Leeds

Multicultural perspectives of music education have been a global agenda since the 1960s in response to the multiplicity of world music cultures worth including in music curriculum (Volk, 1993). Tanzania has at least 120 established ethnic groups, each with diverse musical traditions. These traditions are not only worth transmitting from one generation to the next as a way of enforcing the second educational goal of Tanzania which is "to promote the acquisition and appreciation of the culture, customs and traditions of the people of Tanzania" (ETP 1995, p. 1.), but they are also a rich source of materials for designing children's music activities. Further, music is among the subjects whose learning activities have been incorporated in pre-primary school syllabi in Tanzania since 1995. The musical activities mentioned in the syllabi include: traditional songs, dance, singing games and learning of traditional musical instruments from different ethnic groups.

Despite these efforts, however, little evidence exists on the implementation of these activities in pre-primary schools. This paper reports the findings of a study which recruited 195 teachers from 48 ethnic groups in Tanzania and explored their attitudes toward the importance of music in their communities and in childhood development and learning. It also sought their views and preferences on the recommended musical traditions to be used in pre-primary school children's music activities. The implications and applications of the findings for music educators in Tanzania, and more globally, will be considered.

PAPER: Songs from the crib: toddlers; private bedtime vocalizations: a collective case study

‖ Meryl SOLE

University of New Haven, Connecticut

Research on children's spontaneous singing has shown that children are inherently musical and freely initiate vocal play and improvised songs. These spontaneous vocalizations often highlight experiences and events that are meaningful to the children who sing them. The experiences of toddlerhood are filled with wonder as toddlers begin to walk, talk and make sense of the world around them. Toddlers, who do not yet have the ability to internalize their thoughts often verbalize their thinking out loud in the private moments before sleep. Although evidence of spontaneous singing has been documented in studies during the pre-sleep period, researchers have only interpreted the data from a linguistic perspective.

In this collective case study, I sought to investigate and describe nine toddlers' pre-sleep musical vocalizations. The parents (co-researchers) observed their children twice a week for four weeks. For the first 15 minutes of each observation, the parents stood outside the child's bedroom and described and contextualized what they heard on a researcher-developed form. The parents also collected audio recordings of each session.

Parent/family interviews were conducted at the beginning and end of the study. Each of these types of data were pooled to create profiles of each child and to examine the existence of patterns across cases.

Results showed that all of the toddlers spontaneously vocalized to some degree in their private pre-sleep moments. The observed musical utterances included free-flowing vocalizations, re-working of learned songs and fully improvised songs. In line with the literature on general vocalizations, these toddlers sang to reflect, experiment, learn, express emotion, self-soothe and make sense of their recent experiences. Reflections of communicative musicality were evident in the private reflections of 5 toddlers who sang about musical communications that they shared with their parents during the day. For many of the parents who participated, awareness of their toddler's private singing caused them alter their daily parenting practices to share more music with their children.

Through the simple act of listening, these adults were awakened to what was meaningful to their children. Private song is a vehicle for learning, processing, creating and expressing in toddlerhood.

PAPER: Performance anxiety, self-esteem, self-efficacy and attitudes towards performance in American, Czech and Balkan University music students

▌ Ena STEVANOVIC

Charles University, Prague

Music performance anxiety (MPA) is one of the most frequently reported problems among professional musicians that can cause severe performance impairment and distress, hindering musicians from reaching their full potential as performers. Possible contributing characteristics are low general self-efficacy and low self-esteem. (Sinden, 1999). MPA is a relatively neglected phenomenon in Eastern European literature and is considered to be a personal issue that cannot be researched or influenced by the education system and therefore many gifted students are denied the opportunity to perform due to their anxiety. The aim of this study is to investigate the relationship between MPA, self-esteem and self-efficacy and to examine possible differences in attitudes towards performance between American, Czech and Balkan university music students. Surveyed participants were 53 music students from Croatia, Bosnia and Herzegovina, Czech Republic and the USA. Research data were collected using Rosenberg Self-Esteem Scale, Sherer Self-Efficacy Scale and Kenny Music Performance Anxiety Inventory. Ten participants were also interviewed using a 40 item structured interview in order to examine their attitudes toward performance in their educational environment. Findings suggest that low self-esteem and low general self-efficacy are significant predictors of MPA in all three groups. Persistence and initiative items in the self-efficacy scale are highly negatively correlated with MPA, while there is no significant correlation between the items of effort and MPA. Female participants reported significantly higher anxiety levels than male. American students have higher scores in self-esteem scale, while there is no significant difference in self-efficacy items between the groups. Qualitative analysis shows that all three groups consider insufficient preparation, lack of experience and low self-confidence to be the major causes of MPA, whereas Czech and Balkan students reported more negative experiences in the education system and they tended to blame their teachers for high level of MPA. Implications of these findings for teachers and learners in Eastern European higher education are also discussed.

PAPER: Basic psychological needs satisfaction through instrument learning in childhood and adolescence: a retrospective study of professional classical and jazz musicians

‖ Rachel SWINDELLS

Manchester Metropolitan University

With a focus on professional jazz and classical musicians, this paper presents research which investigated instrument learning through the lens of basic needs theory (Deci & Ryan, 2000). Considering the retrospective accounts of six musicians (three classical, three jazz), it examined the mediating role of autonomy, competence and relatedness needs in the motivation of music-making/learning from early childhood up until entry into higher education. A qualitative research design was employed to generate rich data illustrating how basic psychological needs are satisfied/thwarted in this domain. Narrative interviews were undertaken and subject to a hybrid inductive-deductive thematic analysis. Findings indicate that autonomy needs were met through musicians pursuing intrinsic interests, exerting volition over their training, and developing distinctive musical identities; however, this need appears to have been frustrated in the classical-musicians' earliest music-tuition. Competence needs were satisfied through participation in optimally challenging activities, with an aptitude for music contributing to an evolving musical identity. Relatedness needs were supported through the bonding act of group music-making, but also through identification with teachers, parents, siblings and/or peers. The study concluded that basic needs theory provides a compatible framework in which to understand experiences of music-making/learning, pointing to directions for future research.

PAPER: "Orchestra"- can a symphony really make a change?

|| Lina TSAKLAGKANOU

Institute of Education, University of London

The purpose of this study is to investigate the effect of orchestral music making on the social-emotional and cognitive wellbeing of participants in the National Orchestra for All (NOFA). NOFA, inspired by the El Sistema model of 'Music Education for Social Change', takes a well established idea - a national youth orchestra – and reconceptualises it for young people who face barriers to musical progress and music-making. This research is an 'instrumental' Case Study - a 'real-life' example of how a Sistema-inspired residential music programme might influence young people aged 11- 18 years old. It focuses on change over time with regard to self-esteem, confidence, self-efficacy, musical self-concept and skills, musical development and explores the processes that may contribute to any such change, amongst the orchestra participants. This will be a longitudinal study run over the course of three years. It uses a mixture of quantitative and qualitative methods in order to capture a rich picture of the extent and ways in which NOFA may be a transformative experience for the participants. A pilot study has begun in the year 2014, which will be expanded and redeveloped throughout the following two years. The research will have a direct impact in helping NOFA to achieve its aims. The findings will potentially have wider impact in terms of informing and enhancing the practices amongst other Sistema-inspired programmes.

Society for Education, Music and Psychology Research

PAPER: Portuguese children's musical worlds in the public schools. Why do some children play and other children listen?

❚❚ M.Helena VIEIRA

Instituto de Educação da Universidade do Minho Centro de Investigaçao em Estudos da Criança

Communication can be seen today as a basis for equality or inequality. In times when technology is worldwide spread it may contribute to promote democracy; on the contrary, its absence may accentuate social differences and exclusion. In this sense, schools are ideal for the democratization of all kinds of languages and forms of communication. Music literacy is one of the most powerful of these forms of communication and, as a functional and sequential language it should be accessible to all children through adequate teaching methodologies and well prepared teachers. In the 21st century it is no longer acceptable that some children (in specialized schools, such as conservatories or academies) might have access to learning the music language (performing, reading, writing and composing) and other children (in general schools) have to limit themselves to casual listening and aesthetic contemplation, on the poor excuse of a supposed (and yet to be proved) lack of talent. This presentation tries to trace the origins of the problem, to present today's curricular structure and to suggest possibilities of improvement; so that schools might stop training some children to play and other children to listen.

CONFERENCE PROGRAMME & INFORMATION

University of
Reading

SEMPRE Postgraduate Study Day
Exploring Music Education and Psychology Research

Friday 24 October 2014

PROGRAMME

NOTE: ALL SESSIONS TAKE PLACE IN STUDIO I, MUSIC EDUCATION BUILDING

9.30   **Registration**
[Music Education Office]

9.50   **Welcome**
Dr Mary Stakelum
Conference Organiser

10.00   **Doctoral research: introductory remarks**
Professor Dianne Berry OBE
Dean of Postgraduate Research Studies, University of Reading

SESSION 1   **Research on music teaching and learning**
               FOCUS   *Defining the questions*

10.30   *The formal/informal frontier: learning and teaching where two worlds meet.* Alison BUTLER (Open University, UK)

11.00   *Dots and Lines – Investigating the role of Western staff notation in musical learning in Scotland.* Diljeet BHACHU (Reid School of Music, University of Edinburgh)

11.30-11.45 COFFEE   [Foyer]

11.45   *Secondary school students in instrumental lessons: what motivates them to learn and continue with their instrumental tuition and what can teachers do to support this?* Kate SWINBURNE JOHNSON (University of Reading)

12.00   *Aiming for enjoyment or progression: an investigation into how instrumental teachers use learning objectives.* Lucy BEVERIDGE (University of Reading)

12.15   *What is the backwash effect of instrumental music examinations?* Simon PARKER (University of London, Institute of Education)

12.45- 13.30 LUNCH   [Foyer]

SESSION 2 Researching young children's music making
         FOCUS   Methodological considerations

13.30   *The use of experimental music and classical music in children's composition at of children aged 9–10.* Emma HAWKSLEY (University of Roehampton)

14.00   *"Orchestra"- can a symphony really make a change?* Lina TSAKLAGKANOU (Institute of Education, University of London)

14.30   *Working memory in children's musical practice: preliminary results from an ongoing research study in a Brazilian Child Symphony Orchestra.* Larissa Padula Ribiero da FONSECA Diana Santiago, Jonatas Leal (Federal University of Bahai Brazil)

15.00   *Teachers' attitudes toward using multicultural musical traditions in pre-primary music activities in Tanzania.* Albini Akonaay SARAGU (University of Leeds)

15.30-15.45 REFRESHMENTS   [Foyer]

SESSION 3 Researching performance anxiety
FOCUS   Presentation of findings

15.45   *An investigation into College musicians' musical performance anxiety through selected performance strategies (cognitive strategies, behavioural strategies, and cognitive behavioural strategies) by self-management.* WEI-LIN HUANG (Institute of Education, University of London)

16.15   *Performance anxiety, self-esteem, self-efficacy and attitudes towards performance in American, Czech and Balkan University music students.* Ena STEVANOVIC (Charles University, Prague)

16.45   Closing review

17.00   END
Please note: The conference committee reserves the right to make changes to the programme. This version is correct at the time of release.

sempre:

Society for Education, Music
and Psychology Research

University of Reading

Children's Musical Worlds

Saturday 25 October 2014

Institute of Education
University of Reading

PROGRAMME

NOTE: ALL SESSIONS TAKE PLACE IN STUDIO I, MUSIC EDUCATION BUILDING,
LONDON ROAD CAMPUS

9.30   **Registration and coffee**
        [Music Education Office]

9.50   **Introduction and Welcome**
        Mary Stakelum
        [Studio 1]

9,55-11.15 SESSION 1   'Children's Musical Worlds' Keynote panel

Professor Graham WELCH, (Institute of Education, University of
London) with Dr Evangelos Himonides, (Institute of Education,
University of London), Professor Adam Ockelford (University of
Roehampton), Dr Costanza Preti (University of Winchester), Dr
Jo Saunders (Institute of Education, University of London) and
Angela Voyajolu (University of Roehampton)

11.15   BREAK

11.30-12.30   SESSION 2 Perspectives on musical engagement

11.30   *Private musical worlds: inside the minds of tweens and teens*
             Ruth HERBERT (University of Oxford)

12.00   *Songs from the crib: toddlers; private bedtime vocalizations: a collective case study.* Meryl SOLE (University of New Haven, Connecticut)

12.30 - 13.30   LUNCH, POSTERS and AGM (1pm)

POSTERS

Working memory in children's musical practice: preliminary results from an ongoing research in a Brazilian Child Symphony Orchestra. Larissa Padula Ribiero da FONSECA, Diana SANTIAGO, Jonatas LEAL (Federal University of Bahia)

Writing music inspired by the creativity and fantasy-world of children. Shiva FESHAREKI (Royal College of Music, London)

An investigation into College musicians' musical performance anxiety through selected performance strategies (cognitive strategies, behavioural strategies, and cognitive behavioural strategies) by self-management. Wei-Lin HUANG (Institute of Education, University of London)

Voices and connections: a polyphony of perceptions from the remembered childhood musical worlds of retirement-phase amateur musicians. Janette JOLLY (Institute of Education, University of Reading)

Music and Talent: multiple intelligences development through music. Francisco José Cuadrado MÉNDEZ (Universidad Loyola Andalucía)

Teachers' attitudes toward using multicultural musical traditions in pre-primary music activities in Tanzania. Albini Akonaay SARAGU (University of Leeds)

Performance anxiety, self-esteem, self-efficacy and attitudes towards performance in American, Czech and Balkan University music students. Ena STEVANOVIC (Charles University, Prague)

13.30-15.00   SESSION 3 Modes of representation in responses to music

13.30   *Children's graphical representation of music: Gaining insight into their musical world.* Vicent GIL, (University of Valencia, Spain), Mark REYBROUCK (University of Leuven, Belgium), Jesus TEJADA (University of Valencia, Spain) & Lieven VERSCHAFFEL (University of Leuven, Belgium)

14.00   *Miming stories and playing rhythms along with recorded music.* José Carlos GODINHO (Escola Superior de Educação, Instituto Politécnico de Setúbal, Portugal)

14.30   *Exploring children's understanding of music through the use of drawings and interviews.* Susan HALLAM (Institute of Education, University of London) and Tijia RINTA

15.00   REFRESHMENTS

15.15-16.45   SESSION 4   Approaches to learning

15.15   *Portugese children's musical worlds in the public schools. Why do some children play and other children listen?* M.Helena VIEIRA (Instituto de Educação da Universidade do Minho Centro de Investigaçao em Estudos da Criança)

15.45   *Basic psychological needs satisfaction through instrument learning in childhood and adolescence: a retrospective study of professional classical and jazz musicians.* Rachel SWINDELLS (Manchester Metropolitan University)

16.15   *Musical agency in primary classrooms: The impact of informal learning on 5-6 year old students.* Leslie LINTON (University of Western Ontario)

16.45   CLOSING DISCUSSION

17.00   CONFERENCE CLOSE
Please note: The conference committee reserves the right to make changes to the programme. This version is correct at the time of release.